Greenwich

Sea-power put the Great in Britain and for centuries Britannia's navy ruled the waves. Greenwich on the south bank of the Thames, five miles downstream from London Bridge, is a memorial to the maritime might of the nation.

The Cutty Sark, a Victorian sailing clipper, rests in dry dock on the river bank. Nearby is Sir Francis Chichester's yacht, Gypsy Moth IV, in which he sailed single-handed around the world in 1966-67.

The National Maritime Museum, containing records and relics of 500 years of naval history, is based in the elegant Queen's House. Designed by Inigo Jones in 1616 as a palace for King James I's consort, it is one of the earliest and finest Renaissance buildings in the country. Four-square on the river's edge is one of Sir Christopher Wren's masterpieces; originally in the 15th century a royal palace, in 1692 it was established as a hospital for sailors and in 1872 became the Royal Naval College.

The prime meridian of zero longitude, accepted as the time zone of the world, runs through royal Greenwich Park which rises above the museum. Monarchs through the ages have left their mark on Greenwich and archaeological remains show that the area has been a choice site for settlers since prehistoric time.

1

Tower Bridge

Tower Bridge stands sentinel over the Thames, guarding the heart of London. The most famous and distinctive bridge in London, it raises its twin 1,000 ton drawbridges in salute to allow ships to pass up river. Built in 1894, when Victorian engineering reached its zenith, the bridge is 800 feet long and spans 200 feet between the massive Gothic towers that rise from the river bed. It takes 1½ minutes for the drawbridges to rise. All the original machinery for raising and lowering is still in place with just one concession to modern technology: electric motors now replace the steam engines.

Between Tower Bridge and London Bridge is moored HMS *Belfast*, which saw active service in World War II. One of the largest and most powerful cruisers ever built for the Royal Navy, *Belfast* is now a floating museum.

Until the 18th century London Bridge was the only bridge over the river in London. The present pre-stressed concrete version was constructed in 1967-72. Its granite-faced predecessor was demolished in 1968 and sold and re-erected at Lake Havasu City, Arizona, USA.

2

Tower of London

Tales of torture, treasure and treason make the Tower of London the capital's top tourist attraction. Built to impress and dominate the people of London, it has been an awesome symbol of power throughout its 900-year history.

William the Conqueror began the massive fortress in 1066 from a mound on the north bank of the Thames from which he could command the capital of his newly captive kingdom. Successive kings added to the fortification which has through the ages served as a royal home, repository for the royal menagerie, prison and execution centre.

For centuries the Tower was Britain's most imposing and important centre for historical activity and regal chicanery. Richard II signed his abdication in the Tower in 1399. Henry VIII married Catherine of Aragon in the Tower while he had two other wives — Anne Boleyn and Catherine Howard — executed there. Bishops, statesmen, plotters and poets have all met their end in the Tower. Even in the 20th century traitors have died in its precincts: several spies were shot during the World Wars.

Famous prisoners include Guy Fawkes, who planned to blow up the Houses of Parliament, and Rudolf Hess, Hitler's deputy who spent time at the Tower after his unsuccessful secret flight to Scotland in 1941. Visitors today can view the instruments of execution and torture, an arsenal of weapons, and the nation's treasure, the Crown Jewels. A solemn ceremony, almost 700 years old, is still performed nightly when the Chief Warder of the Tower hands over the keys for safe keeping to the Resident Governor.

3

The City

The modern concrete and glass buildings rearing into the City skyline are monuments to Mammon. This is the heartland of London's money and commercial interests, where venerable old buildings nestle in the foothills of new office blocks.

The City has been bustling with businessmen since Roman times. It occupies a site, 'the square mile', virtually regarded as the whole of Norman London. The area embraces the Bank of England in Threadneedle Street, the vaults which house the nation's gold reserves, the Stock Exchange, and the internationally famous insurance institution Lloyds of London. Chief offices of banks, insurance companies, stockbrokers and mercantile houses jostle for space here.

Historically the area was the centre for the Guilds or Companies set up by tradesmen and craftsmen to boost and protect their own interests. The Weavers Guild was established 800 years ago but most have been in existence since the 14th century. Leading members of many of the 84 Guilds or Companies wear quaint and distinctive costumes or liveries for their traditional ceremonies.

The Mansion House is the official residence of the Lord Mayor of London, who provides pomp and pageantry each year when he rides in a State coach to the Law Courts — a ceremony that dates back to the 14th century.

4

St. Paul's

Sir Christopher Wren's masterpiece stood silhouetted against the blazing skyline during the Blitz of the Second World War. Today its glory is reflected in the glittering glass office blocks which surround and overshadow it. It has an indomitable dignity and grandeur that inspires the nation at moments of great solemnity: the funeral service of Sir Winston Churchill; the wedding of Prince Charles to Princess Diana.

The Gothic cathedral previously on the site was severely damaged in the Great Fire of London in 1666. Wren's classical design for its replacement was accepted reluctantly after much misgiving and muttering over its new-fangled style.

Seat of the Bishop of London and 'parish church' of the British Commonwealth, the cathedral is crowned by a central dome which rises to 365 feet — the largest in the world after St. Peter's in Rome. The building is remarkable for having been completed in 35 years, within the lifetimes of the bishop, architect and master mason involved in the scheme. It cost just under £¾ million to build...£736,752 2s. 3d.

Britain's illustrious heroes — Nelson, the Duke of Wellington and Wren himself — are fittingly buried here. Wren's simple epitaph says: "Reader, if you seek a monument, look about you".

5

The Temple

In days of yore Knights Templars, an order of military crusaders who would now be labelled freedom fighters, made their headquarters in the 12th century in the area known as The Temple. They built their own Temple Church which survives today. It features a circular nave and was styled on the Holy Sepulchre in Jerusalem, a church the Templars pledged to protect from the heathens on their holy crusade.

The present occupants of The Temple site still enjoin battle, but with words not swords. The Middle Temple and the Inner Temple are two Inns of Court, a centre for the legal profession.

The area is an oasis of gardens and graceful buildings including the Middle Temple Hall which boasts one of the finest double hammerbeam roofs in England. Shakespeare's own theatre company is believed to have performed Twelfth Night in the hall in 1602.

Three ships — *Wellington, Chrysanthemum* and *President* — are permanently moored by the Embankment. The *Wellington* is the floating headquarters of a City Livery Company whilst the others are training ships.

6

The River

The River Thames bisects the capital, a life-giving artery pumping 1,357 million gallons of water daily along London's most famous thoroughfare. The Thames stretches for 210 miles and 12 million people depend upon it for their domestic water supply. It is now the cleanest metropolitan river in the world, though 25 years ago it was dead. Today 104 different varieties of fish have been recorded in its depths. In 1983 a salmon was caught by rod and line — the first for 150 years.

The river has been continuously used as a highway since prehistoric times, being the safest and most direct way to travel. The Romans built the first bridge and laid the foundations for London.

While its once-teeming dockland has now declined, redevelopment is breathing life into the commercial river banks, with a yachting marina and floating museum at St. Katherine's Dock and new homes from the redundant London Docks.

One of the most ambitious civil engineering projects ever constructed — the Thames Barrier, crossing the river from Charlton to Silvertown — now protects London from the risk of flooding from the increasing height of surge tides. It was completed in 1982.

Westminster

At Westminster, with the Thames lapping at the walls, are the Houses of Parliament. Built in 1840 on an 8-acre site of a former royal palace, the elaborately carved stone building in Gothic style contains 11 courtyards, 100 staircases and two miles of passages.

The Clock Tower, one of the best known London landmarks, rises to 320 feet. Big Ben is the name of the bell (13½ tons in weight) which is struck each quarter hour. A light in the tower tells that the House of Commons is in session at night.

The Houses of Parliament are steeped in pomp and tradition, ceremony and splendour. The Queen rides in a State coach to Westminster to open each new session, usually in the second week of November. Each day, before business begins, the Speaker of the House of Commons in knee breeches and long black gown walks in solemn procession into the chamber. The Speaker presides over sittings and keeps order.

Westminster Hall is the only remaining part of the mediaeval palace, except for the Jewel Tower and St. Stephen's Crypt. It has been the scene of famous historical trials and state events.

The House of Lords is a lavishly decorated Gothic style chamber containing the throne of the sovereign and the Woolsack, seat of the Lord Chancellor, which by tradition has been placed in the House since the time of Edward III in the 14th century. The House of Commons is more restrained in style, having been rebuilt in 1950 following war damage. The Commons' chamber consists of parallel rows of green leather benches which face the well of the chamber where the mace (a symbol of authority) is placed. By a quirk of overcrowding there are seats for only 437 of the 650 elected members at any one time.

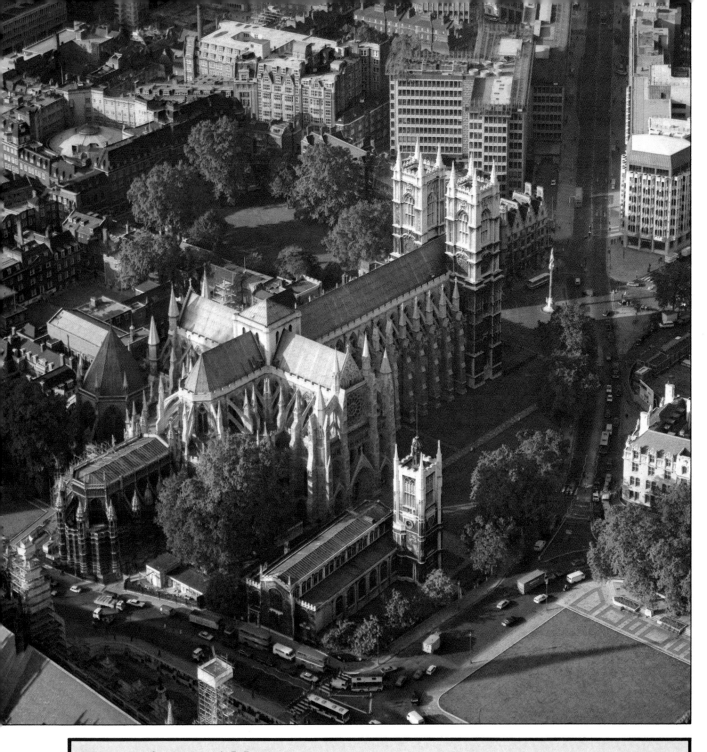

Westminster Abbey

No church in Britain has been so closely connected with the nation's history as Westminster Abbey. Coronations of sovereigns spanning 900 years have been held here; within its walls are buried most of our monarchs and the Chapter House was the meeting place of our early parliaments.

Westminster Abbey occupies a site once known as Thorney Island. Small portions of the building date back to the 11th century, the choir and sanctuary are 13th century, the nave 15th century and the chapel early 16th century. Near to the west door is the best known tomb in the church: the Unknown Warrior, whose body was brought from the battle fields of France and buried in the Abbey in 1920 as representative of more than a million British soldiers who died during the First World War.

The Stone of Scone, a symbol of Scottish royalty, was carried off to Westminster by Edward I in 1296 to form part of Edward the Confessor's Coronation Chair, upon which almost every ruler of England has been crowned.

Lambeth Palace

Within a short stretch of the River Thames, between Westminster Bridge and Lambeth Bridge, two palaces hug either side of the river bank. While the Palace of Westminster (or Houses of Parliament) concerns itself with matters secular, Lambeth Palace is the home of matters spiritual. Lambeth Palace has been the London home of the Archbishop of Canterbury for over 750 years. The buildings occupy the site of a Saxon manor house given to the church by William the Conqueror. Every ten years representatives of the Anglican Church from Britain, the Commonwealth and USA meet here for the Lambeth Conference of Anglican Bishops. The last was held in 1978.

The oldest surviving part is the 13th century Chapel Crypt. Of the old palace, which was attacked by Wat Tyler and his rebels during the Peasants' Revolt in 1381, only parts remain. Extensive damage was caused by bombs during World War II. The Great Hall boasts a magnificent hammerbeam roof, 70 feet high. The library contains many treasures, including illuminated scripts and the earliest printed books. Captain Bligh of the Bounty, best known for his mishandling of the mutiny on board ship, is buried in St. Mary's churchyard next to Lambeth Palace.

Tate Gallery

Sugar magnate Sir Henry Tate who gave the world sugar cubes also gave the nation art. He commissioned the classical building which houses the greater part of the national collection of British painting, and also gave his own collection of more than 60 works.

The Tate Gallery, which faces the Thames, was opened in 1897 on a site called Millbank where a former model prison once stood. The world famous collection includes almost every important British artist since the 17th century, as well as foreign masterpieces and modern sculpture. Extensions have been added over the years to accommodate the growing treasures bequeathed or bought by the Gallery.

While the idea of a national collection of British art was first mooted by sculptor Sir Francis Chantrey, it was Sir Henry Tate who made it possible. The Tate is renowned for its modern works of art and exhibitions, some of which have inspired outraged comment and controversy.

Buckingham Palace

Buckingham Palace is the most famous royal home in the world. Built in 1703, it was bought by George III sixty years later for the bargain price of £28,000. The imposing aura of the palace owes much to its site. Its 'backyard' is a 40-acre expanse of lawns and lake. Despite drastic alterations by Nash and Sir Aston Webb, the Palace still looks like a country house. The sumptuous State Apartments, which are not open to the public, are used for investitures and entertaining visiting heads of state.

Outside Buckingham Palace at 11.30 every morning the famous Changing of the Guard takes place to the accompaniment of the Guards' bands. The Royal Family occupies the north wing of the palace and the Royal Standard is flown when the Queen is in residence.

13

Trafalgar Square — St. James's

From his column, Admiral Lord Nelson gazes over the surrounding buildings onto a sea of green — St. James's Park, regarded as the most attractive in London. It covers 93 acres and was once a marshy meadow, drained by King Henry VIII and converted into a deer park.

Charles I walked across the grass from St. James's Palace to his execution in Whitehall in 1649. The park was remodelled in 1826 when the architect John Nash created the lake where pelicans, ducks and assorted water fowl now live.

The area known as St. James's to the right of The Mall is one of the most exclusive in London. It bristles with the best known gentlemen's clubs — The Athenaeum, Boodle's, White's, Brook's, the Reform — and expensive shops.

Admiralty Arch, which looks as if it embraces traffic entering its portals en route for The Mall, was erected in 1910 as part of the national memorial to Queen Victoria. Behind it along Whitehall is the Ministry of Defence and Horse Guards Parade, where the annual Trooping of the Colour ceremony is performed before the Queen to mark her official birthday.

Trafalgar Square

Named to commemorate Nelson's great naval victory over the French in 1805, Trafalgar Square is a great rendezvous for pigeons and political demonstrations. Four bronze lions, cast from cannon from a sunken ship, lie at the feet of the 167 foot high column.

Nelson looks down Whitehall (foreground) to the Houses of Parliament in the distance. Swivelling clockwise, Admiralty Arch leads onwards to The Mall and St. James's Park and Buckingham Palace. South Africa House fronts the east side of the square; Canada House the west. The classical style building on the north side of the square is the National Gallery, housing one of the richest and most extensive collections of art in the world. In the north-east corner of the square stands the church of St. Martin-in-the-Fields, a classical masterpiece by James Gibbs dating from 1721 and famous for its lunchtime musical recitals.

A fir-tree is set up in Trafalgar Square each Christmas, a gift from the people of Norway in thanks for the hospitality shown to their royal family during the Second World War.

The Post Office Tower

The Post Office Tower, looking like a glass lighthouse in a sea of concrete, is one of the tallest buildings in Britain. Completed in 1964 as part of a telecommunications network, the 580 foot tower with its 40 foot mast rears spectacularly skyward.

From a viewing platform reached by high speed lift the Tower gives a view extending up to 30 miles so that the Chiltern Hills, Windsor Castle and the North Downs can be seen on a clear day.

To the left of the picture is Regent's Park. Originally a royal hunting ground, it was laid out elegantly by John Nash in 1812. Graceful terraces encircle the park to the west, east and south. The 472 acre park is surrounded by a carriage drive 2¾ miles long where fashionable gentry once paraded. An Inner Circle drive, ¾ mile long, encloses the Queen Mary's Gardens containing the open air theatre. London Zoo which houses 6,000 species of animal is also within the park perimeter.

Hyde Park Corner

Hyde Park Corner is estimated to be the busiest traffic island in London. Breasting the road is Apsley House, former home of the Duke of Wellington which bore the most prestigious postal address in town: Number 1, London.

After leaving the army for politics, the Duke became Prime Minister in 1828-30. But his staunch opposition to sweeping social reform made him unpopular. Iron shutters had to be fitted at the 'Iron' Duke's home after rioters smashed the hero of Waterloo's windows. Apsley House is now the Wellington Museum, containing relics of the old soldier.

Fanning out behind Hyde Park Corner is Hyde Park itself. This 360-acre tract once formed part of a vast primeval forest. The Serpentine lake is one of the park's most popular features. Formed by damming the River Westbourne, the Serpentine is a serene 40-acre spread of still water. It is the natural habitat of the hardy bathers who take a dip every morning of the year, as well as numerous waterfowl.

At Hyde Park's Speakers' Corner democracy demonstrates its vitality and diversity, offering anyone the opportunity of jumping on a soapbox and saying what they please.

17

The Museums

One man's vision and verve produced the cluster of museums in Kensington. Prince Albert, consort to Queen Victoria, was the powerhouse behind the establishment of the Science, Natural History, Geological and Victoria and Albert museums. He was the instigator of the Great Exhibition of 1851, a shop window for the best of British skills, ideas and goods. It was a resounding success and the Prince then proposed that the profits be used to purchase land for an array of museums. Building work began in 1856.

The Victoria and Albert Museum is a national collection of fine and applied art. It has around seven miles of galleries with exhibits ranging from the 16th century Great Bed of Ware to ethnic arts and crafts.

The Science Museum has fascinated generations of parents and children with its emphasis on working models that visitors can explore and handle to understand better the nature of invention and technology.

The Geological Museum illustrates the earth sciences with a renowned collection of gem stones, rocks, minerals and fossils which number well over a million specimens.

The Natural History Museum on a four-acre site covers botany, entomology, minerology, palaeontology and zoology, with stuffed animals ranging from an eleven foot high elephant to minute preserved insects.

The Royal Albert Hall

The Royal Albert Hall in Kensington, looking like an upturned jelly mould, is the home of good music from classical to pop.

Opened in 1871, this immense oval amphitheatre is capable of seating more than 5,000 people. Originally acoustically so bad that virtually two concerts could be heard in one sitting — from the echo bouncing back from the dome — modern technology has cured the problem. The Hall's famous organ is one of the mightiest in the world with nearly 10,000 pipes.

Facing the Hall is the Albert Memorial, a sculpture of Queen Victoria's lamented husband Prince Albert.

19

Kew Gardens

What was started as a modest gardening hobby by a Princess has grown into the most famous collection of plants and flowers in the world: The Royal Botanical Gardens at Kew. Situated on the east bank of the Thames, 30,000 varieties of plants and trees grow on the 300-acre site. A further seven million dried specimens are preserved in the Herbarium.

Princess Augusta, mother of King George III, began the garden with the aid of her head gardener in 1759. As the project literally blossomed, despite the original infertile sandy soil, she commissioned little temples and the famous ten-storey pagoda to add interest among the greenery and scenery. The Royal Family gave Kew Gardens to the nation in 1841 and its most important function today is as a scientific institution. Botanists work on vital research as well as identification of plant life. The economic exploitation of plants, which has brought food and industry to developing nations, owes much to the pioneering experimentation at Kew.

The Palm House, a glass and iron construction 360 feet long, was for a long time the largest greenhouse in existence. Designed in 1844 by Decimus Burton, it is home to plants from the tropics of both hemispheres.

Hampton Court

Hampton Court was for many British kings and queens the 'honeymoon home'. On a prime site by the River Thames, it was the grandest of all houses built in Britain in the 16th century. Cardinal Wolsey, one of the most powerful men in English politics, commissioned it with no expense spared. The magnificence and extravagance of the place was just one of the many irritations the irascible King Henry VIII felt concerning Wolsey. Wolsey decided to present his home to Henry as a peace offering but it was too late: in 1529 he was stripped of all his land and belongings and imprisoned for treason. The King moved into the court — complete with his new mistress, Anne Boleyn.

Henry VIII spent large amounts of money on Hampton Court, which became his royal playground. His queens spent much time there and it was the birthplace of Edward VI. Henry's chief works were the rebuilding of the Great Hall, the completion of the chapel and the creation of new royal lodgings. Vast sums were spent on elaborate interior decorations, often carried out by imported foreign craftsmen working by candlelight.

Continued overleaf

21

A closed tennis court was constructed, together with an open air tennis court and three bowling alleys, while to the north of the Palace was the tileyard where jousting tournaments were held.

The Palace was much loved by subsequent monarchs. Mary brought Philip of Spain here for their honeymoon; Charles I brought his child bride Henrietta Maria over the threshold in 1625 and his son also brought his blushing Portuguese bride to Hampton Court.

William and Mary, proclaimed King and Queen in 1689, loved the Palace and made it their prime home. Yet they felt extensive modernisation was needed. Sir Christopher Wren was brought in to revamp Hampton Court into a palace as lavish and stylish as Versailles. As William and Mary were joint sovereigns, Wren had to duplicate the main features of the state apartments, including separate staircases for the King and Queen.

As soon as George III came to the throne in 1760 Hampton Court ceased to be an important royal home. The new King refused to set foot in the place again as it evoked the humiliating experience as a boy of having his ears boxed in public by his father, George II.

The Palace boasts more than 1,000 rooms and is full of treasures, ranging from priceless paintings, furniture and tapestries to kitchen equipment. The gardens have always been a fitting foil to the grandeur of the buildings. Hampton Court is renowned for its formal flower beds, fountains and statues. One of the most popular attractions today is the maze, commissioned by King William after the death of his wife Mary. The State Apartments have been open to the public since 1838, soon after the young Victoria came to the throne.

Eton College

Elegant, exclusive and expensive, Eton College epitomises the English public school system. The second oldest in the country, it was founded in 1440 by King Henry VI.

The school occupies a large part of the town and its buildings are all of different periods. The chapel is one of the finest examples of Perpendicular Gothic architecture and is renowned for its fan vaulting.

The uniform of the boys is probably the most distinguishable and evocative features of Eton College: pupils still wear formal coats.

23

Windsor Castle

Windsor, the largest inhabitated castle in the world, has been a royal home for 900 years. It was one of the first sites chosen by William the Conqueror as a massive link in a chain of castles he wanted to build around London to protect his newly acquired kingdom. Building started in 1070 on an ideal chalk outcrop which reared 100 feet above the Thames, giving a commanding view over the countryside for miles around. In size and plan, the original castle is identical to the present one.

Henry II (1154-89) built the distinctive Round Tower and outer walls. During its nine century history, the castle has been attacked only twice — in 1193 when Richard I was away on a crusade and later when barons rose up against the monarchy, a disturbance which produced the Magna Carta in 1215. Edward III, who was born at the castle, turned it into a more comfortable royal residence in the 14th century. Queen Elizabeth I always regarded Windsor as the safest place of refuge in her realm. Over the ages Windsor has become a repository for the best of

Continued overleaf

British craftmanship, from carvings by Grinling Gibbons, the great 17th century woodcarver, to the exclusive Queen Mary's dolls' house. Produced under the direction of architect Sir Edwin Lutyens, the dolls' house is more than 8 feet long and 5 feet wide and the house and its contents are strictly made to a scale of one twelfth life size. The one inch square books on the library shelves contain poems specially written in them by literary lions G. K. Chesterton and Rudyard Kipling, and painters Munnings and Orpen contributed mini masterpieces to scale.

St. George's Chapel, dedicated to the patron saint of England, is the chapel of the Knights of the Garter. It is a masterpiece of Perpendicular Gothic architecture with its elaborately carved stone vaulting. Henry VIII and his third queen Jane Seymour, Charles I, Edward VII, Henry VI, George V, Queen Mary and many others are all buried here.

Treasures of the castle include arms, armour, furniture, tapestries and paintings by Van Dyck, Rubens, Canaletto, Holbein, Durer, Rembrandt, Poussin and Van Cleef.

The Great Park of Windsor covering 4,800 acres and 14 miles in circumference, was a traditional royal hunting ground. The Great Park is connected to the castle by a straight drive of three miles known as the Long Walk. It was planted in 1685 by Charles II and consisted of 1,650 stately elm trees. Although these were cut down in 1945, the view of the castle from the Long Walk is unrivalled.

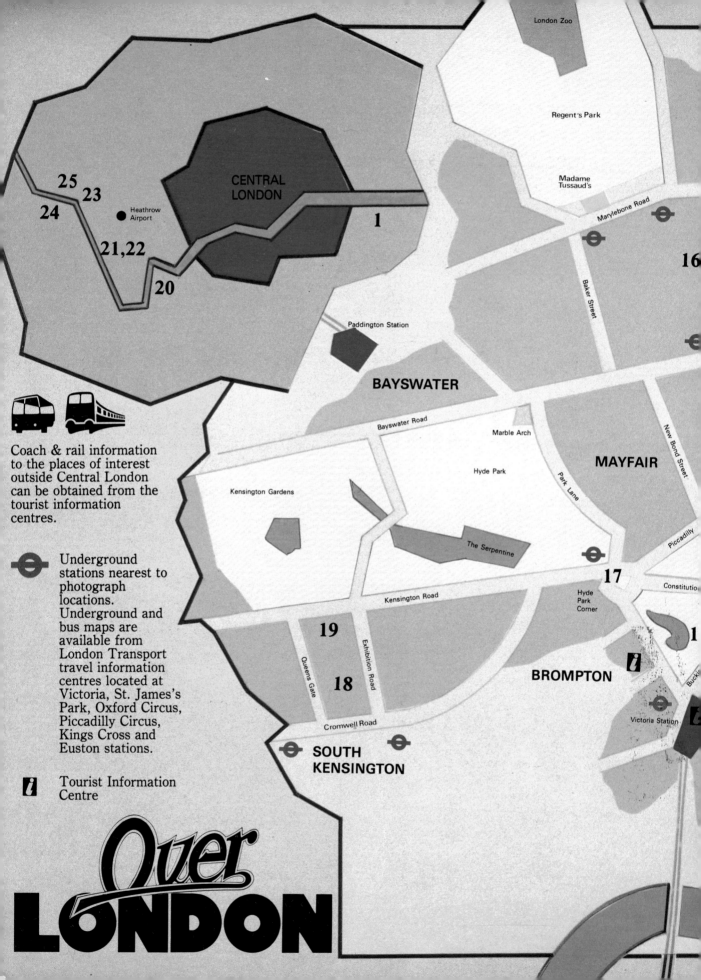

CENTRAL
LONDON

25
23
24
21,22
20

● Heathrow
Airport

1

London Zoo

Regent's Park

Madame
Tussaud's

Marylebone Road

Baker Street

16

Paddington Station

BAYSWATER

Bayswater Road

Marble Arch

New Bond Street

MAYFAIR

Hyde Park

Kensington Gardens

Park Lane

The Serpentine

Piccadilly

17

Kensington Road

Hyde
Park
Corner

Constitutio

1

Coach & rail information
to the places of interest
outside Central London
can be obtained from the
tourist information
centres.

Underground
stations nearest to
photograph
locations.
Underground and
bus maps are
available from
London Transport
travel information
centres located at
Victoria, St. James's
Park, Oxford Circus,
Piccadilly Circus,
Kings Cross and
Euston stations.

19

18

Queens Gate

Exhibition Road

BROMPTON

i

Victoria Station

i Tourist Information
Centre

Cromwell Road

SOUTH
KENSINGTON

Over
LONDON